## A NOTE TO PARENTS

When your children are ready to "step into reading," giving them the right books is as crucial as giving them the right food to eat. **Step into Reading Books** present exciting stories and information reinforced with lively, colorful illustrations that make learning to read fun, satisfying, and worthwhile. They are priced so that acquiring an entire library of them is affordable. And they are beginning readers with a difference—they're written on five levels.

**Early Step into Reading Books** are designed for brand-new readers, with large type and only one or two lines of very simple text per page. **Step 1 Books** feature the same easy-to-read type as the Early Step into Reading Books, but with more words per page. **Step 2 Books** are both longer and slightly more difficult, while **Step 3 Books** introduce readers to paragraphs and fully developed plot lines. **Step 4 Books** offer exciting nonfiction for the increasingly independent reader.

The grade levels assigned to the five steps—preschool through kindergarten for the Early Books, preschool through grade 1 for Step 1, grades 1 through 3 for Step 2, grades 2 through 3 for Step 3, and grades 2 through 4 for Step 4—are intended only as guides. Some children move through all five steps very rapidly; others climb the steps over a period of several years. Either way, these books will help your child "step into reading" in style!

*Special thanks to Maria Marcassa of the Fédération Internationale de Gymnastique for her help. The author and editors would also like to thank Agnes Keleti for her assistance in the preparation of this book.*

**Cover photographs:** Agnes Keleti (A. Keleti); © Bettmann/CORBIS (N. Comaneci); AP/Wide World Photos (O. Korbut, M. Retton, K. Strug).

**Interior photographs:** See cover photo credits above, pp. 1, 3; ALLSPORT, p. 43; ALLSPORT/Russel Cheyne, p. 7; AP/Wide World Photos, pp. 19, 21, 28, 38, 41, 46; © Bettmann/CORBIS, p. 25; © Jerry Cooke/CORBIS, p. 16; Jerry Cooke/*Sports Illustrated*, pp. 30, 32, 37; James Drake/*Sports Illustrated*, p. 22; Agnes Keleti, pp. 8, 13, 15; Al Tielemans/*Sports Illustrated*, p. 45.

www.randomhouse.com/kids

*Library of Congress Cataloging-in-Publication Data*
Bailer, Darice. Solid gold : gymnastic stars / by Darice Bailer.
p. cm. — (Step into reading. Step 3 book)
SUMMARY: A historical overview of notable female gymnasts in the Olympics, including Agnes Keleti of Hungary, Olga Korbut of Russia, and Nadia Comaneci of Romania.
ISBN 0-375-80694-6 (trade) — ISBN 0-375-90694-0 (lib. bdg.)
1. Women gymnasts—Biography—Juvenile Literature. [1. Gymnasts. 2. Women—Biography.]
I. Title. II. Series. GV460 .B25 2000 796.44'082'0922—dc21 [B] 00-027468

Printed in the United States of America August 2000 10 9 8 7 6 5 4 3 2 1

# Solid Gold

# Gymnastic Stars

by Darice Bailer

WITH PHOTOGRAPHS

**A Step 3 Book**

Random House 🏠 New York

# Introduction

Back in the 1970s, a little girl in West
Virginia was driving her mother crazy.
She kept jumping off the furniture,
breaking lamps and chairs! Hoping to
spare the house, the girl's mother signed
her up for gymnastics.

The furniture was saved and, in the
process, a future Olympian was born.
That little girl was Mary Lou Retton. At
the 1984 Olympics, she became the first
American woman ever to win a gold
medal in the individual all-around
competition.

At the Olympics, male and female
gymnasts compete separately. Men
compete in these events: floor exercise,

pommel horse, still rings, vault, parallel bars, and horizontal bar. Women are judged on four pieces of equipment:

*Vault*—The vault looks like a padded bench and stands about four feet tall. Gymnasts run up, leap off a springboard, and push off the vault with their hands. They twist or flip through the air and try to "stick" the landing on the other side. (Points are deducted for extra steps!)

*Balance beam*—Call it a wooden tightrope. The balance beam is not much wider than a sneaker and twice as high as a bed. Gymnasts perform a series of movements along the 16-foot-long beam. They pirouette, leap, and even turn cartwheels into back handsprings!

*Uneven bars*—These are two wooden bars positioned over a yard apart. Gymnasts swing continuously from bar to bar. No stopping is allowed until the concluding landing!

*Floor*—"The floor" is actually a springy mat, 40 feet square. On it, gymnasts perform to music, blending acrobatics and gymnastics.

Six judges rate each athlete. They start by giving each gymnast a score of 9.00—before she performs. After the performance, the judges take off points for mistakes and add points for difficult moves. The highest and lowest scores from the judges are eliminated. The remaining ones are averaged for the final score.

In Olympic competition, the top 12 teams from the World Championships go after gold, silver, or bronze team medals. After the *team competition,* the top three women from each country advance to the *individual all-around,* where their scores from each event are averaged for a final score. Winning the all-around gold medal is a gymnast's dream. It means she's the best in the *world!*

Then the top eight scorers on each piece of equipment move on to the individual competition in that event.

So the next time *you* somersault across the living room, tell your parents you're practicing—for the Olympics! Here are the stories of five gymnasts whose years of training paid off in gold.

# Agnes Keleti

December 5, 1956

Agnes Keleti of Hungary is 35 years old at the time of the Olympic Games in Melbourne, Australia. She's twice as old as the typical gymnast who will compete 44 years later in the Summer 2000 Games in that same country. And she's 14 years older than her competitor for a gold medal in the floor exercise: Larissa Latynina, the 21-year-old Russian champion.

In Agnes's home country, Hungarians have been fighting the Russians for their freedom.

When the Olympics are over, Agnes must decide if she wants to return to

Hungary. Under Russian rule, it's not the same country it was when she was born.

Agnes was born in Budapest, Hungary, in 1921. Then her name was Agnes Klein.

Agnes grew up with an older sister, Vera. Agnes loved to jump and swing, making her father laugh. "You're my little monkey," he told Agnes.

Agnes started taking gymnastics lessons at age four. In 1937, when she was 16, she made the Hungarian National Gymnastics Team.

Two years later, Germany invaded Poland and World War II began. With the world at war, the 1940 and 1944 Olympics were canceled. In March 1944, Germany took control of Hungary.

Agnes was terrified. The leader of Germany, Adolf Hitler, hated Jews. He wanted his Nazi soldiers to get rid of all the Jews in Europe. Like other Hungarians, Agnes carried identification papers with her that stated her religion. *What would happen if a Nazi stopped her and discovered that she was a Jew?* Because she worried for her safety, Agnes bought forged papers that said she was a Christian.

But Mr. Klein, her father, did not. One day, he disappeared on his way to work. Later, Agnes learned that the Nazis had sent him to a concentration camp, where he died. Mrs. Klein and Vera went into hiding at the Swedish embassy in Budapest, Hungary's capital. There they survived until the war ended in 1945. Russian troops freed Hungary from the Nazis, but eventually took control of Hungary themselves.

Agnes returned to gymnastics and qualified for the 1948 Olympics. The Hungarian gymnastics organization changed her last name to Keleti to make it sound more Hungarian.

Three days before the 1948 Games in London, Agnes hurt her ankle and withdrew. She trained for four more years and won three medals at the 1952 Olympics in Helsinki, Finland.

Agnes was 31, but she didn't want to retire. She qualified for the 1956 Olympics—her third! But one month before the 1956 Games, the Hungarians revolted against the Russians. They demanded that Russian troops leave their country and that new government elections be held.

"*Nyet,*" said the Russians. ("No.") Their tanks rumbled down the streets, and

Hungarians fired at them from rooftops. Agnes and her Hungarian teammates escaped to Czechoslovakia and flew to Australia for the Olympic Games in Melbourne.

Agnes was tired of the Russians and war. Vera lived in Australia now. *Maybe,* Agnes thought, *I should too.*

But what would happen to her mother in Hungary? *If only she could get out too,* Agnes thought. Agnes planned to telephone her mother after the competition. Then she'd decide what to do.

Agnes cleared her mind and waited for the judge's signal to begin her floor exercise.

On the floor at the 1956 Olympics, Agnes was graceful and lovely to watch. That was exactly what the judges were looking for—acrobatics *and* beauty.

Despite her age, Agnes tied Larissa for the gold medal in the floor exercise. She went on to win three more gold medals at the Melbourne Games. At 35, she became the oldest gold medal–winning gymnast in Olympic history.

When they finally spoke on the telephone, Mrs. Klein told Agnes that she had sold everything she owned to buy a passport out of Hungary.

That was it. *I am never going back,* decided Agnes.

At the Melbourne airport, Agnes said good-bye to her teammates and cried. It was a sad moment for her to leave her native country behind.

A few months later, Agnes moved to Israel, where she lives today.

# Olga Korbut

August 27, 1972

Olga Korbut doesn't look like the other Russian gymnasts at the 1972 Olympics. They look very serious. But Olga? She's always smiling! The tiny, pigtailed gymnast has quickly become the favorite of millions of television viewers.

During the individual all-around competition, Olga makes the crowd gasp twice. First, over her spectacular somersault high above the balance beam. Then over her uneven bar disaster.

Somersaulting backward off the high bar, Olga reaches for the low bar. She misses and tumbles onto the mat.

Olga's heart sinks, and tears well up in

her eyes. Points will be deducted for the fall. She started the day in second place, but there is no chance of winning an all-around medal now.

Olga cries; then she wipes away her tears. The all-around medals are out of reach, but medals are still up for grabs in the individual events.

Tomorrow, Olga tells herself, she will come back an Olympic champion.

Growing up in Belarus (a country in Eastern Europe that at that time was part of the Soviet Union), Olga had shown that same fighting spirit. She was so small that other children made fun of her. But Olga could run faster and jump higher than most girls *or* boys her age. And she was so light, she could spring like a bouncing ball in gymnastics.

Olga's teachers saw that she was a gifted athlete. At 11, she was chosen to train at the special gymnastics school in her town.

Olga's fearlessness impressed her coach. She was not afraid to try a new jump, twist, or flip—no matter how dangerous it looked.

On the balance beam, Olga could somersault backward. It seemed an impossible feat, since the beam is just four inches wide. Flipping high in the air, gymnasts lose sight of the beam and land where they *think* it will be. And, in competition, they must land without wobbling. *No one could do such a thing, everyone thought.*

But Olga could.

In 1972, at 17, Olga was named an alternate to the Russian Olympic team. She stepped in for an injured teammate at the Munich Games. Then she stepped up to her next challenge—coming back after her fall.

The Olympic crowd is rooting for Olga to make a comeback the following day. And Olga doesn't disappoint her fans. Her back somersault on the balance beam is breathtaking. Her uneven bars routine? Mind-blowing. (And she doesn't fall once!) Olga's floor exercise? Enchanting. In the four individual events, Olga wins two gold medals and a silver, and she wins another gold in the team competition.

Before the 1972 Olympics, gymnastics wasn't that popular. But suddenly little girls around the world wanted to be gymnasts—just like Olga!

Kids rooted for Olga at the 1976 Olympics, and she won a gold and a silver medal. While a new Olympian earned the first perfect score, Olga remained a perfect ten to her fans.

# Nadia Comaneci

July 18, 1976

A 14-year-old gymnast prepares for the 1976 Olympic Games in Montreal, Canada. Her name is Nadia Comaneci. She's from Romania, and not many people have heard of her. Few can pronounce her last name (coe-muh-NEECH).

Nadia looks serious as she readies herself for the uneven bars. Before the games, she told reporters that Olga Korbut came to the Olympics to smile, but *she* came to work. "I want to win a gold medal," Nadia said.

To do that, Nadia must be just about perfect.

But Nadia will be better than that. She

will, in fact, *be* perfect.

Growing up in Romania, a country in southeast Europe, Nadia loved bouncing on furniture. In three years, she broke four sofas. She could not sit still.

Luckily, a Romanian couple came along who could put Nadia's energy to good use! Their names were Bela and Marta Karolyi (kuh-ROH-lee). The Karolyis were starting their own gym. They wanted to train little girls to be gymnasts.

Mr. Karolyi went from school to school, looking for athletic girls.

"Who likes gymnastics?" Bela asked.

Six-year-old Nadia raised her hand.

Nadia performed a perfect cartwheel, and Bela invited her to train with him.

Nadia was determined to become the best gymnast she could be. She practiced

for several hours a day, six days a week. She polished her routines, then took on more difficult moves. When she was eight years old, Nadia won the Romanian Junior National Championship.

In 1974, France invited countries to send their top two gymnasts to Paris for a meet. Bela took Nadia and another gymnast. That year, Nadia was 13. Officials thought she was too young and wouldn't allow her or her teammate to compete.

Bela hid the girls behind a pile of floor mats. After the Russian world champion performed the last vault, he motioned for Nadia to come out and vault.

Nadia threw off her coat and ran to the runway mat. She wasn't afraid to compete against the world champion. Nor was she scared to vault without a trial run. When Bela signaled her to go, Nadia took off. She sprang into a handstand on the vault, twisted, and somersaulted backward.

The crowd was stunned. *Who is she?* the audience wondered. Millions of people would come to know Nadia's name two years later…at the Olympics.

At the 1976 Olympic Games, Nadia whirls around the uneven bars at dizzying speed. She soars into a perfect handstand on the high bar. Then *swoosh!* She swings wide and rockets around the low bar. She shows off three new acrobatic tricks before flying off in a back somersault.

When Nadia's score is posted, the crowd looks puzzled. Only the number 1 is lit.

"Where is Nadia's score?" Bela asks the judges.

An announcer explains what happened. Nadia scored a 10, the highest possible

score. That meant that Nadia hadn't made *any* mistakes. But no one had been judged perfect at the Olympics before—and the scoreboard wasn't made to go that high!

In five days of competition, Nadia scored *seven* perfect 10s. Nadia took home a total of three gold medals, a silver, and a bronze.

She was the youngest Olympic gymnastics champion in history. And she set a higher goal for future gymnasts to achieve: *Perfection.*

# Mary Lou Retton

August 3, 1984

Mary Lou Retton is a tiny gymnast with a huge crowd cheering for her. She's 16 and competing for the United States team at the 1984 Olympics in Los Angeles. Americans wave red-white-and-blue flags, chanting, "U.S.A.!"

WE'RE BETTIN' ON RETTON, a banner reads.

Mary Lou's fans are counting on her to win the gold medal in the individual all-around competition. Mary Lou is determined to do it. It would make her the first American woman ever to win a gold medal in gymnastics. She'd be the best woman gymnast in the world.

But after performing on the bars, beam, and floor, she is not in the lead. Mary Lou trails a girl from Romania—Ekaterina Szabo—by less than one point.

Now Mary Lou warms up for her last event, the vault.

As she does, she peeks at Ekaterina. The girls are in different groups, performing at the same time on different equipment. It's Ekaterina's turn on the uneven bars.

Ekaterina scores a 9.90. Mary Lou's coach, Bela Karolyi, adds up Ekaterina's points. Mary Lou must perform a perfect vault to finish in front. With a 9.95, she would tie Ekaterina for the gold medal. Mary Lou needs to score a perfect 10.

"You have to work now like you have never worked in your life," Mary Lou's coach tells her.

Mary Lou nods. She's ready. She's been ready since she was a little girl!

When she was eight years old, Mary Lou watched the 1976 Olympics on television. She saw Romanian gymnast Nadia

Comaneci win three gold medals.

Mary Lou wondered, *Could I win a gold medal at the Olympics?*

She decided to try.

First, Mary Lou worked hard to become the best gymnast in West Virginia. Next she'd take on the country—and finally, the world!

At 12, Mary Lou qualified for the U.S. Junior National Team. Meeting other gymnasts made Mary Lou realize that she needed a better coach. In order to become the best gymnast in the world, she needed someone who could help her improve— someone who could teach her more difficult skills.

There was a coach named Bela Karolyi. Bela and his wife, Marta, had trained Nadia Comaneci.

The only problem was, the Karolyis

worked in Houston, Texas. Mary Lou would have to move away from home, live with a different family, and go to school in Texas. She was just 14 years old.

But Mary Lou did it. Making the Olympic team was more important to her than anything.

Bela was a tough coach. Mistakes drove him crazy! He wanted Mary Lou to do everything perfectly.

Soon she did.

In 1984, Mary Lou earned a spot on the U.S. Women's Gymnastics Team. But six weeks before the Olympics, her left knee began to ache. It swelled up, and she couldn't walk. A doctor told Mary Lou that she needed knee surgery to remove some bone chips.

Her dream of winning a gold medal now seemed impossible.

But the surgery went better than expected. The doctor allowed Mary Lou to go home and train. He even gave her the okay to compete at the Olympics.

Mary Lou was so relieved! Her knee soon healed, and in July she flew off to the Olympics.

The women's all-around finals came down to Mary Lou and Ekaterina.

After the first round, the two girls were tied. After the second, Ekaterina led—but only by fifteen-hundredths of a point. Mary Lou scored a 10 in her floor exercise, but Ekaterina was still in the lead.

Mary Lou thought she could beat her. *You can do it,* she told herself.

All she needed was one more perfect 10.

Mary Lou wiggles her hands, waiting for the green light that signals that she can go.

*Click.* The light turns green and Mary
Lou explodes down the runway.

She leaps onto the springboard and does

a complete flip and a double twist in the air.

Mary Lou lands and throws her arms up toward the ceiling. *I did it,* she thinks.

"Ten! Ten! Ten!" screams the crowd.

Thirty seconds later, the number 10 lights up on the board. Mary Lou has won!

Bela swoops her up into his arms as the crowd stands and cheers.

# Kerri Strug

July 23, 1996

Kerri Strug is competing at the Olympics in Atlanta, Georgia, for the U.S. Women's Gymnastics Team. The U.S. is in the lead for its first Olympic team medal, but the Russians are close behind.

After competing on the uneven bars, beam, and floor, the Americans move onto the vault. The Russians move onto the floor. As Kerri warms up, she watches the Russians perform. The floor is one of Russia's best events. Her team needs to do extremely well to stay in front.

But one of Kerri's teammates falls on both her vaults. *Is the gold medal now out of reach?*

Kerri is the last American up. She has always wanted to be in the spotlight. And all eyes are on her now. It is up to Kerri to earn the points the Americans need.

Kerri runs, springs up, and somersaults over the vault, but she lands hard and falls. A sharp pain shoots up through her left ankle. When she stands to wave to the judges, Kerri knows she's hurt herself badly. The pain in her foot is unbearable.

Points will be deducted from her first vault. If she lets the first score stand, the Russians will surely get the gold medal. She must make a

second vault, despite the pain.

Kerri limps toward the runway.

*Just let me do this,* Kerri prays.

This is her Olympic moment. The one she's been practicing for since she was a little girl.

As a kid, Kerri pretended that curbs were balance beams and her swing set an uneven bar. She practiced floor exercises in the living room, tumbling from end to end.

When she was six, Kerri watched the 1984 Olympics on television. She wanted to make it to the Olympics and win a gold medal too. If only she could find the right coach.

One day at a competition, Kerri met Bela Karolyi. He and Marta had trained Olympic gold medal winners Nadia Comaneci and Mary Lou Retton. Kerri asked the Karolyis if they would coach her. The Karolyis agreed, and at age 13, Kerri began training with them. Bela and Marta pushed her to be perfect on all the equipment. Kerri got better and better.

At the 1992 Olympics, Kerri became the youngest athlete on any of the American teams. She made no mistakes in her routines, but missed qualifying for the individual all-around by a fraction of a point.

Kerri wanted to prove that she could do better

and win an all-around medal. She kept on training and qualified for the 1996 Olympic team.

Kerri was determined to win a gold medal in Atlanta. But then she hurt her ankle after her first team vault. *How could she and the U.S. team win a gold medal now?*

Kerri shakes her left leg, trying to ease the pain. Her teammates are counting on her. Without a successful vault, there will be no gold medal for the U.S. Women's Gymnastics Team.

When the green light flashes, Kerri runs and somersaults over the vault. She lands in terrible pain, hopping onto her right leg to finish out her vault. Then she falls.

People rush to her side. She'd only finished on one leg. *Would her vault count?*

Kerri asks that question over and over as she is placed on a stretcher.

Kerri is carted to the training room. Suddenly, she hears Bela screaming. "We won!" Bela cries. "Kerri, you did it!"

Lying on the stretcher, Kerri has no idea how she'll walk out and receive the team medal.

Bela steps in to help Kerri. "You just put those gold medals in your country's hands," Bela says. "Even if I have to carry you, you're going out there."

And Bela does carry her out!

# Future Perfect 10s

The 2000 Summer Olympics will be held September 14 through October 1 in Sydney, Australia. Who will be the next Mary Lou Retton? Who will score the *next* perfect 10? Who will win Olympic gold? It could be one of the top three finalists from the 1999 World Championships.

In gymnastics, **Maria Olaru** of Romania is head of the class. Maria won the all-around gold medal at the 1999 World Championships and rarely makes mistakes.

   **Vyctoria Karpenko** of Ukraine missed beating Maria by just *hundredths*

of a point. She's tough and cool, with the talent and desire to be the best.

**Elena Zamolodchikova** of Russia finished third. She'll be tough to beat on the vault. Elena's the world champion in that event!

Who else should you keep an eye on? **Andreea Raducan,** Maria's Romanian teammate. Andreea stole the show at the World Championships. She seemed to float through her floor exercise, barely touching the ground. She earned the gold medal for this event with a 9.837, the top score of the meet.

And don't count out American gymnast **Kristen Maloney,** the 1998 and 1999 John Hancock U.S. Gymnastics Champion. Kristen pulled out of the world finals after spraining her right knee. She still hopes to make it to Australia.